The Heart
of
The Vortex

An insider's guide to the magic and mystery of
Sedona's Vortexes

Richard J. Anderson

Sedona Wind
Publishing

The Heart of the Vortex

First Printing
February 2005

Second Edition
March 2007

Visit our website at www.sedonawind.com

ISBN 978-0-9765897-7-8

To my wife Cindy, who is my guide.

Bell Rock Vortex

Table of Contents

Introduction

Sedona is wonderful, the incredible beauty, the warm friendly people and of course the vortexes! Millions of visitors come every year to Sedona and a good portion of those visitors are here for the vortexes. Maybe they heard them mentioned in a book or from a friend. Or they may have even seen something about them on TV. They felt they had to come and see what it was all about. It was just something they felt they had to do. All too often they have had trouble getting to the vortexes themselves or they didn't know what to do after finding them, so they just "hung out" and left disillusioned. I wrote this guide for those same people. I wanted to empower them so they could get the most from their time at the vortexes without having to stress about whether they are doing it right and so that they could more easily maximize the benefits of the experience. I could have turned this guide into hundreds of pages, but I wanted to keep it simple and direct without giving people too much data to think about. The vortex experience can be natural and joyful with just a little essential preparation.

Please use this guide in a gentle way. Be easy on yourself and don't try to force the experience into a particular pattern of expectation. You might find it very helpful and less of a pain to read most of the book before you even begin to plan your trip, so you're not trying to figure what's what on the trails.

If you just picked this up in a Sedona gift shop and plan on visiting the vortexes right away, please take a little time to digest all the new info and try to keep an open mind.

Enjoy!

The views from Cathedral Rock are gorgeous!

Bell Rock

Snow on the Bell Rock Vortex

Chapter One

What is a Vortex?

Sedona stands out as one of the most powerful places to have a "vortex experience" due to the enormous force found in these gigantic energy points. Sedona is special because of how closely the lye lines intersect and coincide. What also contributes is the composition of the soil. The soil is largely composed of iron oxide, which gives the soil the deep red color and conducts the earth energy more efficiently. In addition, the shapes of the Sedona vortexes help funnel the energy and concentrate it. When you spend time at the vortexes you almost get the impression that they were manufactured for energy conduction, especially Bell Rock.

In the case of Sedona, a vortex is a concentrated area of energy. An area where the energy of the earth is extremely dense and focused in a specific location. The earth generates a tremendous amount of life energy (also called chi or prana) that supports all living things on this planet. The life energy of the planet is more easily experienced in the Sedona Vortexes.

Vortexes can be found in other parts of the world, as well. Some of the more famous areas where vortexes can be found include: Stonehenge, Avebury and Pendle Hill in England, The Great Pyramid, the pyramids near Mexico City and many other areas not quite as famous, but never the less very powerful. Vortexes are often associated with healings, spiritual transformation, mystical journeys, profound states of peace and other metaphysical phenomena. Many of these locations are kept secret from the public at large. That is why we are so lucky to have one of the most powerful vortexes so accessible.

Notes

Notes

Cathedral Rock from Red Rock crossing

Chapter Two

Preparing to visit the Vortexes

This depends on many factors and a lot of it is really common sense. What are the weather conditions going to be like? If it is summer, you should dress lightly, wear a hat and bring plenty of water. If you are going to be at the vortex for less than an hour (very likely if it is your first time, most people have trouble sitting still until they become accustomed to the energy) 2 quarts of water per person should suffice. Remember that Sedona often reaches 107 in the summer months. That is why I always recommend that people visit during the Fall or Spring because the weather is much more moderate and will rarely exceed 80 degrees. No matter what time of the year it is always a good idea to bring at least 2 quarts per person per hour. If you are planning on going for a long hike (as in the case of going to Boynton Canyon, where you have to go on a long hike just to get to the active Vortex center), my advice is to bring 1 gallon of water per person per hour, because you are going to be perspiring more with the exertion. This might sound extreme, but better safe that sorry. More really is better. The air is very dry so it is very

easy to get dehydrated if you don't take precautions. Most people don't realize that Sedona is centered in the middle of a desert!

Other Items you might want to consider is a camera, sunglasses, a good hat that will keep the sun off your head, neck and face, a notepad and some crystals or jewelry that you might want to "charge" or "clear" (more on this later) at the vortex. Also a backpack or fanny pack would be a good idea, because you definitely want to keep your hands free as you walk. Keeping your hands free is really essential because most of the Sedona red rock areas are composed of decomposing, loose sandstone and you may need to use your hands to stop your self from falling if you lose your footing (face it, if you visit the vortexes often your going to lose you're footing sooner or later, it happens to everyone). Another important thing to remember is using the proper shoes. Running shoes with good tread are okay, but I recommend you spend the extra money on a nice pair light hiking shoes or a high quality cross-trainers from a major manufacturer. It if it seams like too much of an investment you could try to find and outlet center in your area or visit a surplus store.

Always bring something to snack on when trekking out to the vortexes so you don't end up focusing your entire attention on food! A few ideas would be: trail mix, string cheese (only if it's not too hot, you don't want to get food poisoning!) energy bars without ginseng (ginseng can too stimulating for many people, especially on the vortexes) Nuts (roasted will stay with you longer), raisins, crackers, beef or turkey jerky, soy nuts, fruit and dried fruit, even a sandwich or 2 would be great if you had some way of keeping it cool.

I always advise people to bring something warm to wear in case the weather changes quickly or you just start to feel cold from sitting in one location for a while. A good light jacket (heavier in the winter) with some weather proofing and Thinsulate (a thin high performance insulating material) would be great. It's important to have some weather proofing material (or water resistant), so that at least your upper body would stay dry if it begins to rain. If it's in the Fall or Winter think about wearing some polypropylene underwear or some similar material that is very thin, but lets your skin breath.

A cell phone is a really good idea in case of an emergency situation, if you are not so addicted to using it that you spend your whole vortex time talking on it. I've never had an emergency that required me to use it, but I've been lucky. What if your car doesn't start when you are finished at the vortex?

Don't forget to get a Red Rock Pass from the visitor center in town or from a ranger station. The Red Rock Pass is essential to traveling on National Park Lands. If you don't display one on your car in a conspicuous location you could end up with a costly ticket when you return to your vehicle. The fees help maintain the Sedona park lands for everyone. It will cost you $5 a day, $15 a week or the best deal, $20 a year.

Having a "Vortex experience" means you are going to be sitting in one place for quite a while and it is essential to be comfortable, and have your mind at rest, so you can stay relaxed and get the most out of you Sedona Vortex experience.

Equipment that is essential* or could be useful:

- A water resistant jacket that "breaths"
- A Red Rock Pass*
- A good hat*
- Light hiking shoes
- Camera
- A small Backpack or fanny pack
- Plenty of water*
- Snack Food*
- A small mat, cushion, or pillow so you stay comfortable
- A notebook
- A small first aid kit
- A cell phone* in case of an emergency.

Notes

Notes

On the trail to Bell Rock

Chapter Three

Getting the most out of your Vortex experience

There are several things you can do to maximize your vortex experience. The first is to do your best to leave your typical and habitual thought patterns and conceptions behind. Allow yourself to temporarily let go of what's consistently going through your mind. Remind yourself that you can always address those "important" issues when you get back to your car. Heavy rational thinking can interfere with your time at the vortex and hinder your ability to let go. An effective way for most people is to try to shift your focus towards your senses without the commentary of your mind. It sounds difficult, but it's really isn't, it's a choice that might require a little practice.

You want to find a comfortable location not too close to a well traveled path. You want too find a quiet, private place where people wont stop and discuss what you are doing. This won't always happen, but when it does it can be very distracting. Look around the area and exercise your intuition (everybody has it even you) and see if you aren't drawn to a particular location. Try not to think too much about it and use your feelings to guide you to an area to spend some time. Maybe an area looks especially beautiful to you, an area that seems to be calling you. It doesn't hurt to have a great view either, so you might want to keep that in mind.

Get comfortable in the vortex area on your pad, close your eyes and notice your breathing as it flows in and out. Feel it as it fills your lungs. Notice when it appears to stop and reverses before you exhale. Keep your attention on that point when your breath reverses for a few minutes, watching your breath. Do this for a few minutes with your eyes closed. Next, open your eyes and do your best to "rotate" your attention through your senses. Start by trying to put all your attention on what you are hearing for a few minutes, then "rotate" all of your attention on what you are seeing. Then "rotate" to the physical sensations of your skin for a few minutes and then return to your breath again and notice as it flows in and out. Don't try to control the experience and don't try to control your breath, try to have the attitude of a relaxed, focused attention during this exercise. Don't try to control the direction of your thoughts, either, just be aware of them and watch them. Be an observer, not a judge. The whole exercise should take you about 15 minutes with a result of quieting your mind. Remember not to judge your thinking or your physical sensations during the process or you will become tenser instead of becoming more relaxed. Allow it be okay no matter what you are thinking or feeling during this process.

Doing this simple technique will open you up and make you more receptive to the wisdom and insights in the vortex area.

I also think that it's a good idea to say a little prayer of protection, like "Father, protect me" or "Universal Spirit, surround me" and imagine a brilliant light surrounding you. If you believe in masters, guides or angels, you could also ask them to be with you and guide you during your vortex experience. I don't want to scare people, but you are going to be in a receptive state and it is a good idea to take the proper precautions.

Bell Rock looking North on 179

Another thing you can do is to avoid alcohol or recreational drugs of any kind within a few days of visiting the vortex. Use common sense and continue to take the drugs prescribed by your doctor, even if you are going to the vortex for a "healing" type experience. That said, there is one drug that I use while visiting the vortexes, and that is caffeine. I enjoy a good cup of coffee and I don't stop when I visit the vortexes, but I don't over do it. If possible, drink half of what you usually do and you might have a better time. Excessive coffee can cause heart palpitations, make your mind race and make it difficult to stay in one spot very long. Coffee is a motivator and it can make it more of a challenge to quiet your mind and receive the most from your time at the vortexes. Many popular coffee chains make their coffee so strong that it's like having a pot of coffee in one cup. If you are highly addicted to coffee, have a little before you go and remind yourself that you can drink as much as you like when you're done at the vortex.

Take it easy when visiting the vortex, enjoy yourself, try to stay in the moment and let it all happen the way it's happening, naturally. Don't force anything! If you become angry, allow yourself to be angry without inflicting it on anybody. If you are blissful, be blissful. The point is not to try to fight what you are experiencing. The vortex is taking your mental, spiritual and physical body to a higher state and this may cause a "clearing out" process. A clearing of the old, stagnant way of being.

It is always best to go with at least one other person. Choose people that will allow you to be natural. You want to be with people that are open to the whole vortex phenomena, people that you can sit still with and that can keep quiet for a period of time. You don't want to bring anyone with you that will make fun of you or your desire to visit a vortex. Also, this definitely not a good time to get to know someone, or to kindle a romance.

A little about Reiki

I'm a Reiki Master myself and encourage people to take a Reiki I class in their area by a qualified instructor. Being "attuned" by a Reiki master aligns you with a universal healing energy that surrounds all of us. It is not difficult being attuned and anyone that has a desire to balance and heal themselves and others, should look into it. Reiki is a powerful healing system and expands your ability to derive even greater benefit from your time at the vortexes. Being attuned in the Reiki tradition is not essential to visiting a vortex, but the experience is definitely more powerful. Being attuned activates your own vortexes in your body and the effect is compounded when going to Sedona. Giving or receiving Reiki on the red rocks is incredible. Just something for you to consider.

Notes

Notes

The Heart of the Vortex

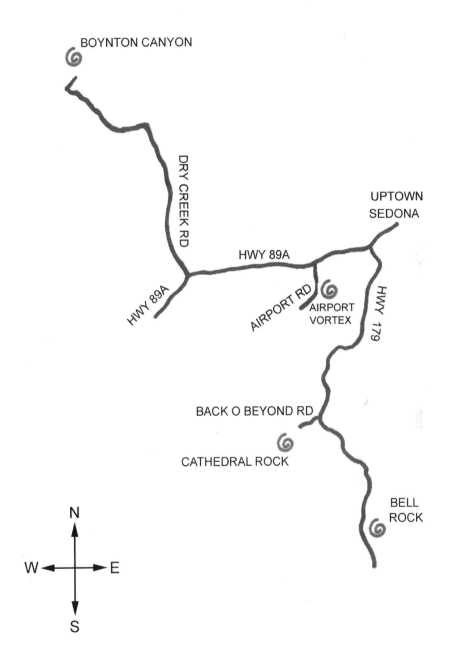

Chapter Four

Getting to the vortexes

Just being in Sedona is being in a vortex, because the whole place is a vortex. But the energy is even more concentrated in 4 main areas, called the vortexes:
- Bell Rock
- Cathedral Rock
- Boynton Canyon
- Airport Vortex

Some lesser known and perhaps less dramatic in their effects are:

- Coffee Pot Rock
- Schnebly Hills
- Courthouse Butte
- The Chapel of the Holy Cross

The so called "lesser" vortexes are not discussed in any detail in this guide. You can find them located on an area map and I encourage you to check them out for yourself.

Courthouse Butte

Courthouse Butte is not considered to be a vortex, or to have any special forces connected with it, but it is stunningly beautiful none the less. The trails around the area are wonderful to explore and provide many spectacular views.

33

The Chapel of the Holy Cross

A mushroom shaped rock in the Schnebly Hills

Coffee Pot Rock

Courthouse Butte

Bell Rock

Bell Rock is my favorite vortex and one of the most powerful. Take HWY 179 South from Uptown Sedona, after traveling about five miles you will see the unmistakable bell shaped rock on the left. Try to park as close to the vortex as possible in the designated areas, but be extremely careful. People drive way too fast on this road and parking can be treacherous if you are not careful. Grab your gear and find the clearly marked dirt trail that leads from the parking area closest to Bell Rock and take it towards the vortex. Contrary to what most people think, you don't have to go to the top of Bell Rock to have a great vortex experience. The vortex draws energy up from the entire area and sitting at the bottom of the rock can be very powerful. I have a secret area that I like to use right at the base. When you are at the base, where the national park trail begins, there is a short trail into a little cubbyhole to the right. I have had some of my most powerful experiences in the area towards the back.

Cathedral Rock

The easiest way to Cathedral Rock is to again take HWY 179 South about 3 miles and make a right on Back O Beyond RD and travel about a mile down this road until you see the parking lot. Walk up to the base and find a comfortable area to meditate.

Another way to get there, and perhaps a more scenic route is to take HWY 179 South, past Bell Rock into the City of Oak Creek, you will want to make a right turn on Verdy Valley School Road. And follow the road about 1/2 of a mile and it will turn into a dirt road. Follow this for approximately 2.5 miles, until you reach a small, clearly marked, parking lot on the left, park here. At this point you will have a clear view of Cathedral Rock (as seen in the photo above). You'll have to walk north on the dirt road that you were driving on until you see a guard rail, at this point you'll want to veer to the right and follow the trail east for about ¾ of a mile, or so, and you will find yourself in large clearing, look for an opening in a barbwire fence to the right. This is the Baldwin

Trail. Follow this trail to the base of Cathedral Rock. You do not have to climb high on Cathedral Rock to feel and absorb the energy. I have to tell you that this vortex is one of my favorites, because the energy, in my opinion, is a very profound and peaceful. Try it out for yourself though and see what you think. There is no doubt that the views in the area are incredible, so you will definitely want to bring a camera.

Airport Vortex

The Airport Vortex is relatively easy to find for most, but requires walking up a very steep grade to the top, for about 100 feet. You might not want to try it, unless you are in good condition, because of the high altitude in Sedona. To get there follow the 89A freeway west from downtown Sedona, about 1/3 of a mile and make a left turn at Airport Road. Take it up the winding road, about 300 feet and park at the first parking area to the left. Walk up the decomposing sandstone, until you see the beautiful vista of the Sedona valley (you can stop here if you are not in very good condition, and find a place to sit). Now turn to the left and carefully make your way up the sandstone, about 40 feet until you come to a flat area about 100 feet wide, this is considered to be the heart of the Airport Vortex. I love this place, the energy is invigorating and soothing at the same time. Try to spend at least an hour here to get the full benefit. It's not difficult spending time here, as the view is magnificent. This area has steep cliffs, so I can't stress enough, BE CAREFUL!

Boynton Canyon

The Boynton Canyon Vortex is very powerful, but to really feel it you are going to have to walk over a mile into the canyon itself and spend some time there. It is well worth it though, I brought many vortex skeptics here and they left as believers. An added treat is the gorgeous red rocks and if you look closely you can see ancient Indian ruins towards the top of the cliffs. To get to Boynton Canyon, go west on 89A, about 3 ½ miles from Uptown Sedona and make a right at Dry Creek Road, follow the road about 5 more miles until you come to the T shaped intersection (Boynton Pass Road), and make a left and make a right at the next T shaped intersection (Boynton Canyon Road), travel a few hundred feet and find the national park parking lot (if you keep going you will end up driving into the resort). You can find the dirt trail leading north into the vortex from the parking lot. Take the trail into the canyon past the resort on the left. When you've walked about 1 hour or 1 ½ miles find a quiet and private place to sit and soak up the energy. If you see a well traveled trail leading up towards the side of the canyon even better, as there seems to be more concentrated energy toward the side of the canyon. But for preservation reasons, please don't create any new trails. This is a very rigorous walk so take it easy unless you are in excellent physical condition. Remember you are close to 5000 feet in elevation here and you're taking a trail that is rocky and uneven for a large part of the walk. Also keep an eye out for falling rocks from above.

Notes

Notes

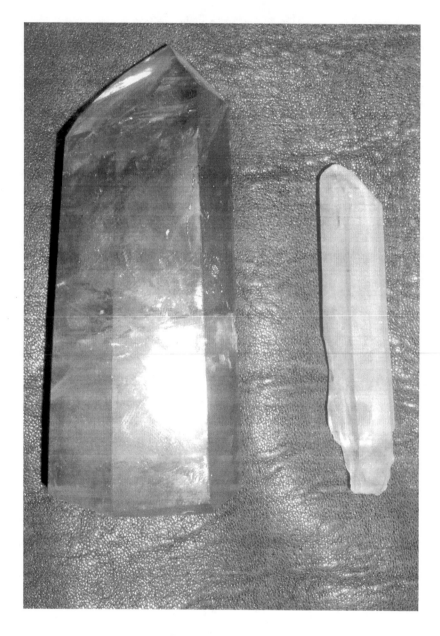

Quartz Crystals

Chapter Five

Charging crystals at the vortexes

A lot of people like to bring stones, jewelry or crystals to the vortexes to charge or cleanse them. Crystals seem to be the best choice for holding and radiating a charge. I recommend that you cleanse a crystal to remove physic residue before attempting to charge it at a vortex. Some people feel just having it in the vortex area cleanses it during the charging process, so it's your choice.

Choosing a crystal

Always use a crystal that you have an affinity for. The crystal can be a foot long or an inch long depending on your preferences and needs. I personally prefer quartz and amethyst for charging and feel they are best choices overall for vortex work. A crystal doesn't have to be free of cracks or have a perfect configuration, but if the cracks appear to go all the way through the crystal it may have tendency to come apart with time and handling.

To cleanse a crystal

You need a container of salt, a glass or a large jar depending on the size of the crystal. Use ¼ cup of salt to 2 cups of water and mix them together thoroughly. Put your crystal in the solution for 3 days or 8 hours if you can put the solution and crystal in direct sunlight, for most of the day. Also it wouldn't hurt to say a little prayer over it asking the great spirit to purify it. Do this process before you leave for Sedona and then wrap your crystals in a nice peace of soft leather or natural fabric, then secure it with a rawhide strip for traveling to the area.

To charge a crystal

Put your crystal in small canvas bag or wrap them in a handkerchief and place them next to you when spending time at the vortex. It is not necessary to have them exposed to the sun.

Also I don't recommend burying them somewhere at the vortexes and coming back at some other time. You might forget where you put them or someone else may find them. Another consideration is that you don't want to accelerate erosion of these beautiful areas. Can you imagine what will happen if thousand of visitors start burying crystals for charging? The whole area would suffer severe environmental damage in a few decades.

Notes

Notes

The view from the Airport Vortex is magnificent!

Chapter Six

Raising your energy frequency

I was going have this as part of Chapter 4 Getting the most from your vortex experience, but I have so much information to share that I felt it deserved its own chapter. By increasing your energy frequency you can more easily align yourself with the higher frequencies of the vortexes and have an even richer experience. These are just suggestions that you might want to try for yourself as an experiment, and see if they work for you as they have worked for me. Don't try to do them all at once or you might just add to your overall stress at the newness of the vortexes. Some of this information may seem very strange to you the first time you hear it, so try to keep an open mind, try it out if you like, and see if it works for you.

Everything in the universe is vibrating at different frequencies. If you raise the frequency of your energy the quality of your life will improve tremendously!
If you lower the energy frequency of your body, you may get sick, depressed, or attract bad luck. You can easily raise the frequency of your body's energy in many ways.

Eating for the Vortexes

First of all, I'm not going to say you have to be a vegetarian to visit the vortexes. I eat some meat and feel it's an excellent source of complete protein. I don't eat large amounts however and I don't eat it every day. I go by how I feel and sometimes my body just craves meat so I have some. I do feel that food has certain vibrations though and if you eat higher vibrational food you can raise your vibrational frequency. Meat has a slower grounding energy. You actually may feel slower, have less energy, be less sensitive to your environment and be quicker to anger when eating beef. I have found that chicken, fish, eggs and cheese have less of this effect so you might want to eat more of these sources of protein when visiting the vortexes.

Raw green vegetables have a faster more pure energy that increases your body's frequency. Some good sources are Romaine lettuce, Spinach and especially wheat grass (juiced). Try eating more of these and see how you feel.

Many fruits have a high pure energy and are well tolerated by most. Some of my favorites are apples, grapes, oranges and grapefruit.

Nuts and seeds are wonderful for your energy, so you might want to try these also, if you haven't already added these to your diet after reading the daily news. Some great ones are walnuts, pecans, brazil nuts (in moderation due to the high selenium concentration) cashews and sesame seeds.

Don't fast at the vortexes! Many people think fasting is a good idea when visiting the vortexes because of the spiritual aspects of fasting. I don't think you should do this because it could be dangerous at a vortex. If you get dizzy when your blood sugar drops to low and you're in an area where you could easily fall or loose your footing it could be a fatal decision. It's also likely that if you're fasting your mind will be on food instead of being at the vortex and taking advantage of the present moment. Fasting is fine if you are in good health and your environment can be completely controlled, like on your couch at home.

Vitamins and herbs also have energy qualities, so they deserve some mentioning here. I take a good multivitamin that is high potency, plus some moderate amounts of general supplements, such as alpha lipoic acid, vitamin E, and vitamin C.

I never take mega doses of supplements because I feel they can unbalance your system over all. Specifically try not to take high doses of the B vitamins (unless prescribed by a physician) because they can speed up your thought processes, and that's not really what you want to do at the vortexes.

Herbs can be great as natural medicines, but I personally only use herbs with medicinal qualities if I am trying to treat a condition. I know I'm going to take some heat for this but I don't take herbs on a
daily basis, and I don't recommend taking them unless they have been prescribed by a qualified practitioner. Herbs are natural and do come from the earth so they may have fewer side effects that chemically produced drugs, but they can be very powerful in their effects.

Herbs such as ginseng and kava should particularly be avoided at the vortexes because of their effects on the central nervous system. Kava works like a natural valium and can have a dulling hangover effect. Asian ginseng can definitely make you feel over energized, especially if mixed with caffeine. If you're going to use ginseng, try the Siberian variety as it has all the powerful adaptagenic qualities without the rush. Our whole point here is to keep your mind as clear as possible, so you can focus your attention.

Sleeping Well

It just makes sense to get plenty of sleep, but people often miss needed sleep, especially when traveling on vacation. You'll find that getting plenty of sleep (7-9 hours for most) will definitely increase your energy frequency, while depriving yourself will of course slow you down and make you less open and aware of the energy changes at the vortex. Depriving yourself of needed rest could have you returning home thinking all of this vortex stuff is crap.

Thinking Well

There is no doubt that your thoughts affect your health and energy level. I also believe they have a powerful affect on the course of your life. But what I'm addressing here is your general thinking at the vortexes. Try not to empower negative thinking at the vortex. The vortexes are sacred high energy spots and you don't want to desecrate them with negativity. When something is really troubling you and you are really upset about it, it may seem impossible to be able let go of the negativity you're carrying.

In this case I would say a prayer such as "Father protect me and purify me" or something similar and imagine yourself bathed in a powerful white light. Don't try to actually fight your negativity by forcing yourself to think positively by sheer will power. Allow yourself to be a silent witness to your thoughts and give them space to be as they are and they will change naturally. You'll find they gather more momentum by resisting them.

Use these techniques before and during your time at the vortexes, and you might have a more profound experience over all.

Notes

Notes

A sacred rock structure in San Diego

Chapter Seven

Finding a Vortex in your area

I wrote this chapter for those who may never visit Sedona and its vortexes, and for those who want to continue their vortex experience when they return home from Sedona.

It is very likely that you can find a vortex in your home town or city. Mankind has been on this planet for quite a while now and always needed sacred places to go to pray or commune with the sacred. Often these areas were used for puberty or fertility rites. They may not have some of the sheer power of the Sedona Vortexes, but over time you can experience some of the same effects if your patient.

You could even find one in the busiest parts of your city. Many times people were just intuitively attracted to a particular spot and felt the town should be there and others arriving would also feel comfortable and energized being there. I currently make my home in the San Diego area and feel San Diego's old town is one of those places. You feel an energizing, soothing energy being there for any length of time, if you are even slightly sensitive to your environment (many aren't though because of excessive and habitual thinking). Another example would be areas of South Pasadena in the Los Angeles Area. Also there is no doubt that Santa Barbara has some of these qualities to some degree. The only problem is that it is harder to find a place to be by yourself and meditate in these areas, unless you happen to live there. Also the air quality is a real consideration because you may want to do some deep breathing as part of your routine.

It really is best to get out and find an energy vortex in the country where the air and other aspects of the environment are naturally going to be better. Look for hills or mountains that seem to naturally draw you and that seem particularly beautiful or appealing in some way.

Local reserves and county parks are often a good choice. Do a little research in your local library and look for sacred areas. Areas that the local or indigenous people have frequented over the years. Always get permission on private land though, never trespass!

Often the energy in vortexes is highly focused in certain locations that you have to be sensitive to. These rather precise locations have often been marked by indigenous people from the past. You just have to be open to the signs and develop a certain sensitivity to your environment as past visitors have over the years.

The best way to know for sure if an area is an energy vortex is to test it. How do you feel there? A positive vortex is distinguished by the calming quiet feeling you'll feel inside. You will feel more centered there. I have found that despite what people think you will feel like you want to relax at a vortex and stay a while. If you feel a sudden force of energy and feel immediately energized it is likely that this is a negative energy vortex and it could be harmful to you. Get out of there! Earth energy vortexes that are good for you are going to have a soothing uplifting energy that slowly builds up in you and nurtures you. The energy from a positive vortex restores and invigorates you, but it is not a frantic energy like a rush from a double espresso on an empty stomach.

Sometimes a small shallow cave in sacred areas, if you can find one, is the perfect place to immerse yourself in vortex energy. I found such a place while on a trail in Northern California. I noticed it while following the flight of an enormous hawk. It was situated about 100 ft above the canyon trail and it was a bit difficult and dangerous to reach, but I felt really lucky to have found it. The view from the cave was breathtaking and I spent considerable time bathing in the soothing energy. It was worn smooth from years of use and had a distinct bowl shape that cradled my back as I sat cross legged in meditation. I'm sure it had been used for countless centuries by shamans of the area.

Of course I don't recommend climbing 100 ft up a rock face to visit a shamans cave because you could easily be killed if you fall. I just wanted to make a point that if you keep your eyes open and your mind receptive, you will find some fantastic sacred locations.

A sacred area in the California Desert

When looking for a vortex or sacred location, look for signs of frequent visits by man or animals (animals are naturally drawn to the energy because it is comforting to them) over the years. Some signs could be a well worn path, where the grass is not growing as thick as in surrounding areas. There could also be signs of Native American influence, such as carvings on the rocks or even rock paintings. Please make an effort to never disturb any signs of early American influence or remains when visiting a sacred area. If you find an unknown Indian settlement always let the local authorities know, so it can be preserved and studied.

If you are sure that you have found an energy vortex, you might also want to say a prayer of thanks and protection. It's really a good idea and it shows respect for the area and for all those who have honored the area over the years. An area that you find could have been used by indigenous people for thousands of years! You can bet that any area you find has been utilized before, even if it was in the distant past and was forgotten. It was much easier for less technologically advanced people to locate an energy vortex. They were more sensitive to their environment because they had a lot less distracting influences and to survive they had to be in tune with the landscape.

You might want to try another way that I sometimes find helpful, if you don't feel too ridiculous trying it out. When in the country, stop and squint your eyes and turn your head from side to side, slowly and patiently. See if you notice an area that seems to be brighter than the rest of the surroundings even though it is bathed in the same amount of sunlight. Carefully move in that direction (if it is within walking distance). When you are in the general area, use the technique again to narrow down the perimeter of the vortex. This can also be effective for finding the center and most powerful part of the vortex. This is definitely a technique where practice makes perfect.

If you have metaphysical beliefs that include spirit guides or angels you might want to ask for their help in locating a vortex.

A good time to get in contact with your angels or spirit guides is a few minutes before falling asleep. Begin by imagine yourself surrounded and bathed in a brilliant white light (another color such as blue or golden could also be used) of protection and clearly state to yourself "Please show me a power vortex in my area". Do this every night for a few weeks and you will be surprised by the results. Often an area will be shown to you in dream. Be open and aware to the results and you will get an answer. Often the answer will come within the first few minutes of awakening before your daily mind has completely turned on. Be receptive throughout the day as you might be given the information through some other unexpected source. This technique is also very powerful for other important questions you need answered in your life. Life's answers really are available to you, if you ask in right way.

Notes

Notes

A view from the Airport Vortex

Chapter Eight

Manifesting at the Vortexes

If you can keep an open mind for a little while, I'd like to share a few things about manifesting in the vortexes. Some of this information will seem almost like science fiction, but you probably wouldn't be reading this book if you weren't at least a bit of a seeker and a little open to the possibility of new realities. Read this if you want to go deeper into the metaphysical aspects of the vortexes. I have found these ideas to be true for me and others that have looked a little deeper. If you only want to get energized at the vortexes and have a fun time, skip this chapter.

You attract what you focus on

Have you ever noticed that when you talk, or think about a particular subject a lot, you tend to notice it more in your environment? Of course you have! Everyone has if they think about it a little bit. Maybe you were going to buy a certain brand of mountain bike, had been giving it some thought and suddenly you started seeing it everywhere. Maybe you thought "that's such a coincidence, I was just talking about that same bike"

I believe it is much more that a coincidence. I feel that people attract to themselves what they focus on consistently over a period of time. I'm going to go a step further here and say that people create their lives, and further more are responsible for everything they have in their lives. They are responsible for all the content they have attracted to themselves.

The idea that we create the fabric of our lives has been out there for a while and many think it is just another "new age" idea and that it will pass. I don't think it is just an idea that will fade with time. Just the opposite, I think it will gain momentum as the years pass. The reason this idea will not pass away is because it's true and can be demonstrated by anyone who gives it a little attention and focus.

How could people possibly create their lives?

I'm going to go a little deeper into metaphysics here so please bear with me. I know that there is an intelligence underlying all things and this intelligence encompasses and supports all things in the universe. This force creates the universe and all things in the universe. You might want to call this force God or you could call it universal life energy, or anything along those lines, but it would just be a label for reference anyway, because this force

68

can't be adequately described with language. For now, let's just refer to this force as Universal Spirit.

This Universal Spirit has no limits and is in everything you know. It is in you, it has to be because it is unlimited. It's in every cell and atom, and behind every thought you think. The amazing thing is that you have this force, this power in you, and that through focus, you can manifest what you desire in your life through this Universal Spirit once you align yourself with it!

If it's in me, why don't I have what I want?

This force is constantly responding to our focus and mental patterns. I feel that we diffuse this force though our thoughts, beliefs and lack of focus. We simply have beliefs and thoughts contrary to our desires and block them from showing up for us. Without focus and a little discipline our goals and dreams will rarely manifest in a way we want. Instead of getting what we want, we often get what we fear, because we keep way too much attention on our fears, hoping they won't happen. This Universal Spirit is always with us and creates what we focus on, whether it is good or bad for us! It's called free will.

The trick is to align our thinking, feeling and visualizations with our goals. If we do this, we will start to get what we want from our lives and our lives will be more fulfilling in the ways we choose. If you dwell on this a while I think you will begin to notice something inside you that agrees that this is true.

What has this got to do with the vortexes?

The Sedona vortexes are more perfectly aligned with this force to a very powerful degree. They will often help to focus and align you to this force to a much greater degree than you can do on your own. You could almost call these locations masters because of the powerful high frequency energy they radiate. Simply by spending time at the vortexes, you will start to vibrate at a much greater energy frequency and this will make it much easier for you to be more aligned in your focus and intentions. You could almost compare the average person's mind to a tangled ball of string that needed to be "untangled" before it can work properly. Immersing yourself in a vortex field for period of time will have the wonderful effect of "untangling" you.

The art of manifesting

The best way to start would be to get comfortable at the vortex and use the technique on page 21 to help you reduce the mental clatter. Then focus on a few items that are important to you and that you would like to see show up in your life.

It may be helpful to you to write them down in a way that easily defines them, without being to wordy and complicating it more than is necessary.

Some examples would be:

I am open to receive joy in my life.

I am open to a satisfying romantic relationship and attract the perfect man/women to enjoy life with.

Money is good and more and more prosperity is flowing into my life now.

I am a lucky person and great things are showing up in my life more and more!

I am now free of the past and choose to create a wonderful joyful life.

My relationship with my husband/wife is growing in wonderful and delightful ways.

I am courageous and able to make the necessary changes in my life.

I am now in control of my destiny.

I claim my healing power and it flows through my body now.

I am a beautiful, wonderful person and I love myself.

I have a wonderful fulfilling life.

Feel free to modify these affirmations to match your way of thinking, so that they seem perfectly suited to you. Remember to keep them in the present tense, because your real power flows from the present moment. When you really think about it, the present moment is really all you have to work with, isn't it.

When you have your selected affirmations, you could hold them in your hand so you could look at them from time to time if needed. Close your eyes and attempt to see the actual reality of your affirmation as if it is happening right now. Hear what you would be hearing, see what you would be seeing and feel the emotions you would be feeling. You could even imagine what you would be touching. There may even be a certain odor you might want to associate with your intention.

Some people have an easier time getting the impression without actually seeing anything. Do your best to see it as well as you can and to make it as clear as you can in your mind. Don't stress over this and try to have a light attitude about the whole thing. Don't make it an "I have to get this right" situation, which will just interfere with the process and block you. From my experience people get better and better at mental visualization and focusing over time. Give yourself a break, after all most people have no real experience focusing their attention.

Try to work on only a few areas at a time, say it in your mind and see it. The more focused you are and the less mental objections, the faster your goal will show up for you. If you find yourself arguing with the affirmation in your mind like "this is stupid" or "this could never happen" bring your awareness to this immediately without arguing with the negative thought.

Your daily conscious mind often produces these kinds of objections because it thinks it's trying to help you. It thinks it's better to have things stay the same and know what's coming rather than face the unknown reality even if it's much better and filled with joy. Acknowledge the minds attempt to keep you "safe" and declare "I am now open and willing to create a new and better life" or something along those lines. Be courageous and persist in your affirming and visualizations and your conscious mind will eventually become more aligned with the new reality you intend to create and stop fighting you.

Persist and you will achieve what you see in your mind and affirm with conviction. Your intentions may not pop into your reality immediately at the vortex but they will show up in time if you maintain your focus. When you return home take your attentions with you to continue focusing on. There will be a time when you might very well find yourself saying something like "wow that's weird, what a coincidence".

This technique is not just for the vortexes (although the effect of being in a vortex field will enhance and accelerate the results) and you can use it anyplace where you can get quiet and center yourself. Write the following statement in your heart so you don't forget. **You attract in life what you focus on**. There's no getting around this, it's just the way it is.

For those who want to explore this further, I have included a varied collection of carefully scripted affirmations in the appendix.

Notes

Notes

Looking north towards Cathedral Rock

Chapter Nine

Otherworldly happenings in Sedona

The Sedona Area is famous for strange happening and the locals don't usually want to discuss them. If you hang around the area long enough you'll have some of your own stories to tell, but you might want to keep them to your self.

Some of the most common phenomena described include:

Unidentified Flying Objects (especially in the vortex locations), including actual saucer shapes, and strange lights at night. Unusual and otherwordly visitors. Voices that seem to come from nowhere. Past and future life experiences. Dramatic and spontaneous healings.

I don't want to talk about my personal experiences to any degree, because I don't want to "lead your perception" I feel if you are focused on a particular event you might tend to draw that into your awareness. Which is something you may or may not want to do.

I will say that it is very likely that if you invest a degree of time at the vortexes it is extremely likely that you will experience such profound states of peace and emotional refreshment that it can definitely be classed as metaphysical.

Notes

Notes

Recommended books

There are many great books to assist you in your vortex quest and for general self development. These are a few of my favorites.

1) The Power of Now by Eckart Tolle
This is an amazing book by a living master. We are very fortunate to have this book available to us and I always recommend it. It deals with the issues of transcending our conditioned and limited minds.

2) The Power of Silence by Carlos Castaneda.
This is a wonderful book for shaking our basic belief systems and opening ourselves up to a new way of being.

3) You Can Heal Your Life by Louise Hay.
Louise reveals the truth that our lives are the result of what we consistently think about.

In conclusion

I hope you enjoyed this little guide and that it has been helpful to you. I enjoyed writing it and taking the photographs. Remember your inner guide, it will give you insightful information if you ask often, are patient and practice listening.
Peace

About the author

Richard Anderson is a writer, photographer, artist, poet, intuitive, Reiki master and experienced Sedona vortex guide. He has been guiding groups to the Sedona vortexes for many years.

Appendix

Affirmation scripts

The following pages are some of the scripts I developed for my CD programs. Use them at the vortex or in meditation. You may purchase these in subliminal format at www.sedonawind.com

I Am a Confident Person

I am a confident person.
I can do anything.
I love myself.
I have the strength and power.
I make wise choices.
I am attractive.
I am skillful.
I have great power within me.
I am the master of my life.
I have a deep knowing that I can achieve my
dreams.
I have a deep knowing that I can achieve my
goals.
I am very self confident.

I Can Lose Weight Now

I can lose weight now.
I am beautiful.
I am now healthy and attractive.
I love myself.
I love the way I look.
It's easy for me to stay healthy and attractive.
I choose healthy foods now.
It's easy for me now to be slim and attractive.
I allow myself to be slim and attractive.
It is good. I respect myself.
I am happy.
Good things happen to me.
I deserve it

© 2005 by Richard J. Anderson

I Am Very Lucky

I am a very lucky person.
I attract wonderful things.
Wonderful things happen to me all the time.
I deserve wonderful things in my life.
I feel a wonderful inner joy.
I am a wise person.
My intuition is strong and defined.
I am open and receptive to good things in my
life.
I am very fortunate.
I deserve a great life.

I Look Young and Beautiful

I look young and beautiful.
My body renews from within.
My body is strong, fit and beautiful.
My cells are full of healthy energy.
I feel wonderful and love life.
I feel and look younger.
I love the way I look.
I notice how much younger I am looking.
My muscles are firm and strong.
My skin is firm and vibrant.
I radiate a healthy glow.
I drink plenty of water and eat healthy.
I get the exercise I need.
I love to exercise I love and respect myself.
I have a great attitude about life.

I Can Be Healthy

I can be healthy.
My body has powerful healing energy.
My healing comes from within.
I can choose a powerful healing.
The perfect energy that created me now heals
me.
The divine dwells within me and heals me.
I am loved.
I love myself.
Of course I can be healthy.
Good things come to me now.
I powerfully attract good things.
Everything is fine now.
I forgive everyone.
Today is a great day.
I feel love.
I am completely open to a wonderful healing.

I Am a Successful Person

I am a successful person.
I am very successful.
I am insightful.
I am lucky.
I am happy now.
I am powerful.
It's great being successful.
I am wise.
I am very confident.
I make the right choices.
It's easy for me to reach my goals.
I write my goals down.
I spend time visualizing my goals.
I see the achievement of my goals in my mind's
eye.
I open myself to success.

© 2005 by Richard J. Anderson

Radiant Prosperity

I create the income I desire.
I appreciate my life.
I am thankful for what I have.
I am prosperous.
I am prosperity.
I love my life.
I am open to prosperity.
I am prosperous now.
It's safe to be prosperous.
My life is wonderfully prosperous.
I am wise and make good choices.
Money is good.
I am happy and healthy.
I love life.
I love myself.
I am loved.

True Self Esteem

I love the way I am now.
I love the way I look.
I am loved.
I feel love.
I am wonderful.
I appreciate myself.
I am very resourceful.
I can handle any situation.
I am powerful.
I am in charge of my life.
I make wise choices.
I am beautiful, whole and complete.
I am healthy.

The Perfect Relationship

I am in tune with my soulmate.
It's time for my perfect relationship.
I am intuitive.
I am receptive to love.
I am loved.
I can express my love.
I recognize my soulmate.
I am powerfully attracted to my soulmate and
my soulmate is powerfully attracted to me.
I am ready for a completely satisfying
relationship.

© 2005 by Richard J. Anderson

Great Job Interviews

I am happy.
I love people.
I know exactly what kind of job I want.
I am lucky.
I prepare myself easily.
People love me.
People appreciate me.
I appreciate myself.
I am very capable and learn easily.
I am smart! I adapt quickly.
I am filled with confidence on interviews.
I get the job I want.
I believe in myself.
There are plenty of great jobs that I can do.
I have a great appearance!
I am a great communicator.
I am very aware of my talents.
I am wonderful.
I am energetic.
I am very capable.
I have a great attitude.
Life is great!

I Love to Study

I love to study.
I am healthy.
I take care of myself.
I feel great enjoyment when I study.
I learn easily.
I am intelligent.
I am quick, clever and smart.
I absorb my lessons easily.
I have a great memory now.
My mind is sharp.
I remember what I need to remember.
I am confident in class.
I am a good communicator.
I am a superior student.

Live From Love

Love is the answer.
I radiate love.
I choose love and peace.
Love flows from within.
I open myself to love.
My heart is filled with love.
I greet life with love, peace and joy.
Love creates miracles in my life.
Love is healing.
Love is abundance.
I live from love.
I am joyful.

Spiritual Warrior

I see things from a higher perspective.
I am strong.
I am powerful.
The power of the universe flows through me.
Negativity falls away.
I am disciplined.
I feel a strong connection to the universe.
I feel a oneness with the universe.
I am well.
I only use my power for good.
I love myself. I feel love.
I am very intuitive.
My senses are clear and sharp.
I am a force for good.
My body easily adapts to a higher energy level.
As I store power my energy frequency
increases.
My high energy frequency protects me
from all negativity.

© 2006 by Richard J. Anderson

Powerfully Creative

I feel the creative flow.
It's wonderful being creative.
I am powerfully creative.
I am full of wonderful creative ideas.
My mind is wonderful!
My creativity is wonderful!
I am a creative person now.
I am intuitive.
I easily create.
My creativity is there when I need it.

The Heart of the Vortex

The Heart of the Vortex

The Heart of the Vortex

Made in the USA